I0776625

November 26

The 330th day of the year (331th in leap years).
There are 35 days remaining until the end of the year.

by Michael Dobson

Timespinner
Press

Table of Contents

For the definition of "O.S.," "CE," and "BCE" used with some dates , see the section "On Names and Dates."

Cover: Golden mask of Pharaoh Tutankhamum in the Egyptian Museum. (Photo: Carsten Frenzl, CC BY-SA 2.0). Archeologists Howard Carter and Lord Carnavon entered the tomb on November 26, 1922 — the COVER STORY and EVENT OF THE DAY.

Quote of the Day

"If the first woman God ever made was strong enough to turn the world upside down all alone, the women together ought to be able to turn back and get it right side up again! and now they is asking to do it, the men better let them."

Sojourner Truth, ex-slave, author, and activist
died November 26, 1883

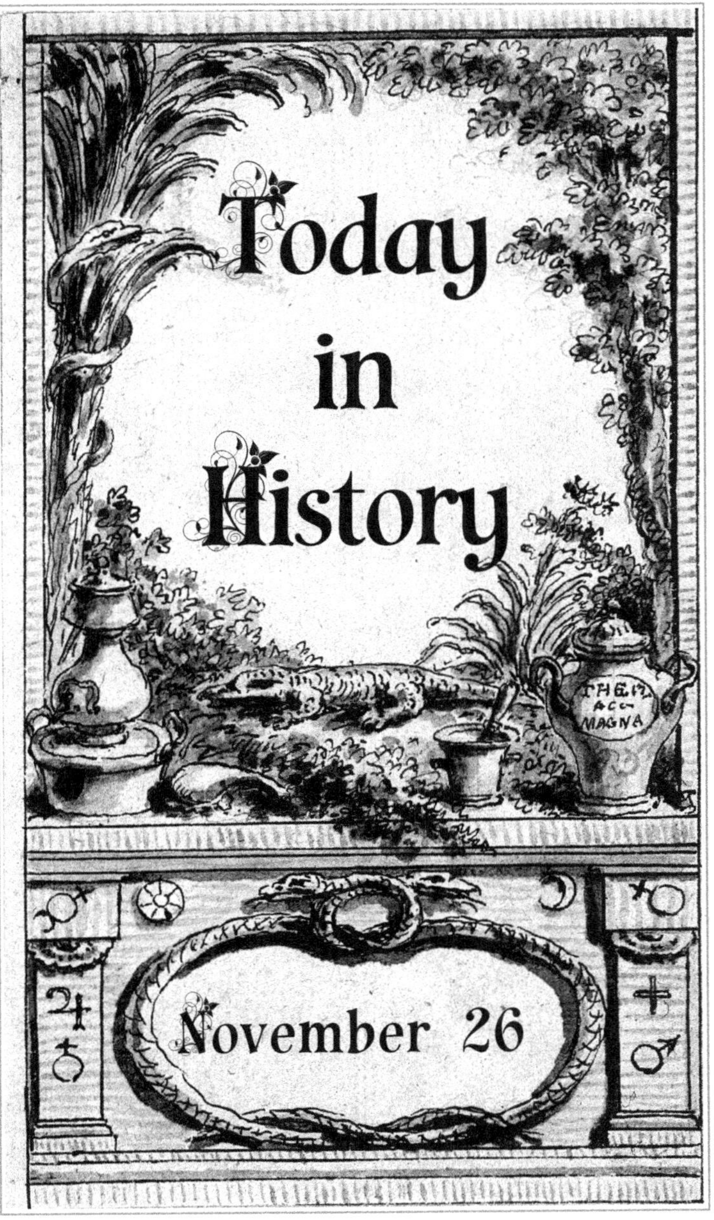
Today
in
History
THERIACA MAGNA
November 26

Labors of the Months: November, by Simon Bening

What Happened on November 26?

While some days of the year are more famous than others, every day of the year is filled with important, exciting, and unusual events, from religious awakenings to natural disasters, from wars to breakthroughs in technology, and from tragedy to triumph.

In this section, you'll learn about all the events that make November 26 important, including the special event that makes up our cover story or event of the day. Some events you may already know about, others may be new to you, but all of them are important parts of the history of the work.

Let's explore some of the reasons why November 26 is a very special day!

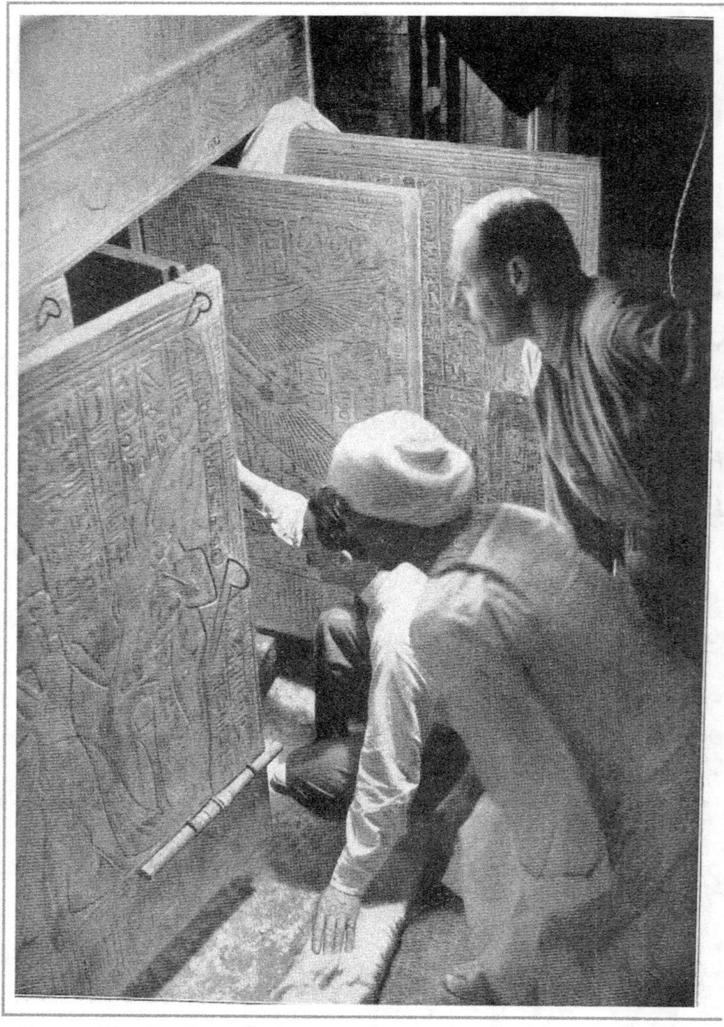

Howard Carter (kneeling) opens the door to the tomb of Pharaoh Tutankhamun, November 26, 1922. (Photo: Harry Burton)

Event of the Day/Cover Story
1922 - King Tutankhamun's Tomb Entered

On November 26, 1922, archeologists Howard Carter and Lord Carnevon unsealed the doorway into the tomb of Pharaoh Tutankhamun, and peered in. "Do you see anything?" Lord Carnevon asked. "Yes, wonderful things," Carter replied.

Lord Carnevon began sponsoring Howard Carter's Egyptology research in the Valley of Kings in 1914, though the work was interrupted by World War I. By 1922, however, Carter had found little, and Carnevon was ready to withdraw his support.

On November 4, 1922, though, Carter's explorations paid off. His excavation group found a set of steps. Further digging uncovered a doorway, and on November 26, Carter "made a tiny breach in the top left hand corner" of the door using a chisel and peered inside with the light of a candle.

Many tombs had long since been raided for their treasures, but Carter could see a number of items in between two sentinel statues, with another doorway beyond.

It took several months just to go through the treasures in the antechamber, and it was not until February 16 of the following year that Carter was able to open the second doorway. Inside he found a burial chamber containing the sarcophagus of Tutankhamun. It was the best preserved and most intact pharaonic tomb ever discovered in the Valley of Kings, with nearly 5,400 items recovered.

Tutankhamun (generally referred to by the simpler "King Tut") became Pharaoh at the age of nine, sometime around 1332 BCE. His reign lasted approximately ten years. The cause of his death is unknown, but researchers believe it was due to a chariot accident. He left no direct heir.

While he is known to have restored diplomatic relations with neighboring kingdoms, the inscription on his tomb says that Tut "spent his life in fashioning the images of the gods." A number of monuments and temples were created at his direction.

King Tut's tomb was small for a pharaoh, probably because his unexpected death meant his royal tomb was uncompleted. There were two early attempts to rob his tomb, but soon it was buried in stone chips from later tombs, and forgotten.

Although rumor has it that a "Curse of the Pharaohs" killed many of its discoverers, only eight of the 58 people present at the opening died within a dozen years, and one survived nearly forty years.

Relics from King Tut's tomb have been exhibited around the world. The 1970s *Treasures of Tutankhamun* tour was seen by nearly ten million people worldwide. Although Tut's golden sarcophagus was removed for exhibition, his linen-wrapped mummy was left in the tomb, in a climate-controlled glass box to prevent further decomposition.

King Tut was not an important pharaoah in his own right, but today he is one of the best known pharaohs thanks to the tomb discovery. In popular culture, songs ranging from 1923's "Old King Tut" to Steve Martin's 1978 single "King Tut" have been written about him.

The entrance to the tomb (Photo: Harry Burton)

Howard Carter in the burial chamber next to the sarcophagus of
Pharaoh Tutankhamun (Photo: Harry Burton)

More November 26 Events

From the creation of great works of engineering and art, to devastating wars and natural disasters, thousands of years of history have left their mark on each and every day. Here are some more important events that occurred on November 26. (Illustrated items are shaded.)

1476 — Vlad III **Dracula,** the historical ruler whose name became synonymous with vampires, defeated an Ottoman army to become Prince (Voivode) of Transylvania for the third and last time. He is killed the following year.

1789 — President George Washington proclaims a national **Thanksgiving Day** for the first time. *(See page XX for more on Thanksgiving.)*

1825 — The **first college social fraternity,** Kappa Alpha, is founded at Union College, Schenectady, New York.

1863 — President Abraham Lincoln makes **Thanksgiving Day** a national holiday, celebrated on the final Thursday of November. *(See page XX for more on Thanksgiving.)*

1917 — The **National Hockey League** (NHL) is founded, with the Montreal Canadiens, the Montreal Wanderers, the Ottawa Senators, the Quebec Bulldogs, and the Toronto Arenas as its first members.

Vlad the Impaler

1942 — The film *Casablanca*, starring Humphrey Bogart and Ingrid Bergman, has its world premier in New York City. It goes on to win three Academy Awards, and remains near the top of lists of the greatest films ever made.

Screenshot of Humphrey Bogart in *Casablanca*

1965 — France becomes the sixth country to place an **artificial satellite in orbit** with the launch of *Astérix*, named for the popular comics character.

2003 — The **Concorde** supersonic passenger plane makes its final flight, over Bristol, UK.

The final flight of the Concorde (Photo: Adrian Pingstone)

Quote of the Day

"Why do people always expect authors to answer questions? I am an author because I want to ask questions. If I had answers, I'd be a politician."

Eugène Ionesco, playwright
born November 26, 1909

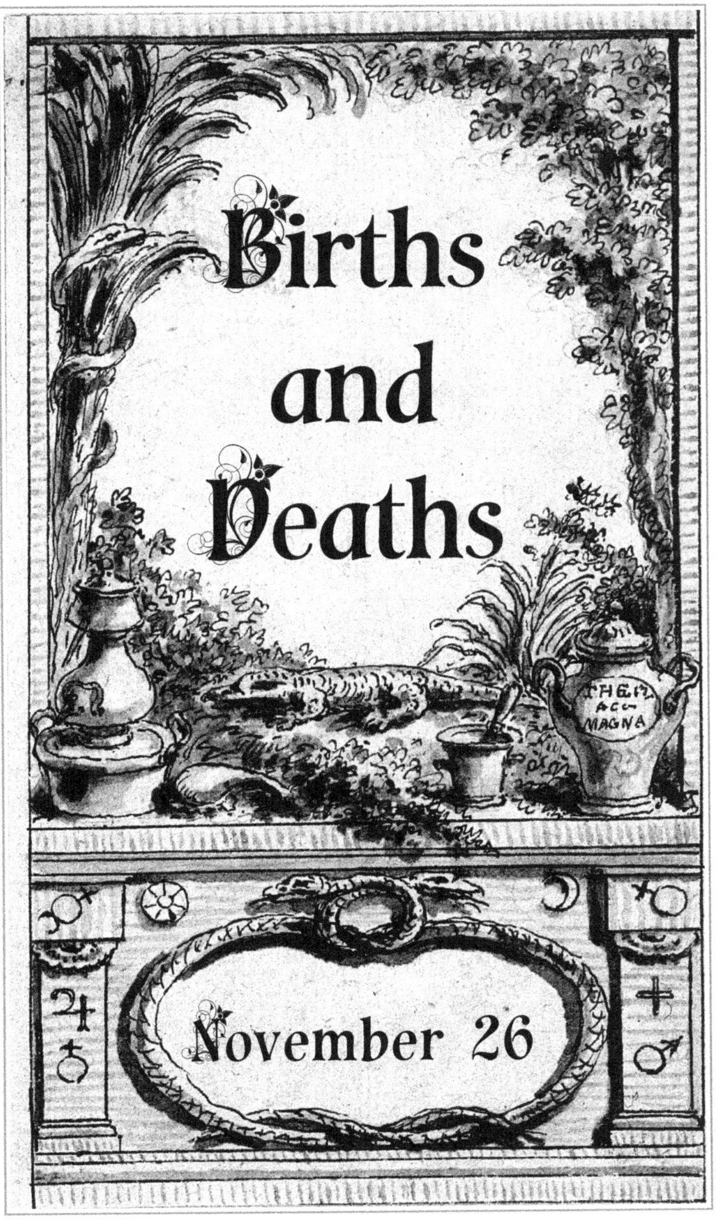
Births
and
Deaths
November 26

Sojourner Truth, abolitionist and women's rights activist. She died November 26, 1883

Notable November 26 People

With the current world population at about seven billion people, on average about 19 million people also celebrate their birthdays on November 26 — and that isn't counting millions and millions who came before! No matter when you were born, you share your birthday with many special people whose accomplishments (and occasionally embarrassments) have been noted as part of history.

In this section, you'll meet fascinating people who share your birthday, or who died on this day in history. They're organized by what they're famous for, and then in reverse chronological order from most recent to earliest. Those who are shown in photographs or artwork have a box around them. We don't have photos of everyone, so please forgive us if your favorite person is missing.

Some of these people you've heard of, others will be new to you, but they all make up an important part of the reason that November 26 is a truly special day!

Saint Katharine Drexel, born November 26, 1858

Who Was Born on November 26?

Art and Illustration

Roz Chast, cartoonist who has published more than 800 cartoons in *The New Yorker. (1954)*

Charles M. Schulz, considered one of the most influential cartoonists of all time; best known for the comic strip *Peanuts. (1922)*

First published *Peanuts* comic, October 2, 1950 (© 2005 United Features Syndicate)

Business

Maurice McDonald, co-developed and opened the first McDonald's fast food restaurant. *(1902)*

Crime and Punishment

Richard Hauptmann, convicted and executed for the abduction and murder of the infant son of Charles and Anne Morrow Lindberg in one of the most sensational crimes of the 20th century. *(1899)*

Bat Masterson, legendary figure of the American West, co-leader (with Wyatt Earp) of the "Dodge City Peace Commission." *(1853)*

The Dodge City Peace Commission. Standing, left to right: W. H. Harris, Luke Short, **Bat Masterson**, W. F. Peillon. Seated, left to right: Charlie Bassett, Wyatt Earp, Frank McLain, and Neal Brown.

Education

Henry Dunster, Puritan clergyman who became the first president of Harvard College. *(1609)*

John Harvard, clergyman who left half his estate to the "schoale...to bee built at Cambridg shalbee called Harvard College." *(1607)*

Military and War

Alice Herz-Sommer, Jewish pianist and music teacher, survivor of the Theresienstadt concentration camp who became the second-oldest known Holocaust survivor at the time of her death at the age of 110. *(1903)*

Dr. Mary Edwards Walker, surgeon and spy for the Union Army during the American Civil War, captured after crossing enemy lines. First and (currently) only woman and one of only eight civilians to receive the Medal of Honor. *(1832)*

Mary Edwards Walker (Photo: George Grantham Bain)

Literature and Journalism

Frederik Pohl, pioneering science fiction writer and editor who won four Hugo Awards and three Nebula Awards, named a Grand Master of the Science Fiction Writers of America; member of the Science Fiction and Fantasy Hall of Fame. *(1919)*

Eric Sevareid, CBS news journalist and commentator; first to report the fall of Paris to the Germans in World War II. *(1909)*

Eugène Ionesco, French avant-garde playwright and a leading figure in the "theater of the absurd." His best-known work is the 1959 play *Rhinoceros. (1909)*

Music

Natasha Bedingfield, English pop singer-songwriter whose first album, *Unwritten*, sold more than 2.3 million copies worldwide. Listed by VH1 as one of the "100 Greatest Women in Music." *(1981)*

John McVie, bass player for John Mayall and the Heartbreakers and Fleetwood Mac, to which he contributed the "Mac." Member of the Rock and Roll Hall of Fame. *(1945)*

Tina Turner, singer-songwriter and dancer whose many hits include, "River Deep—Mountain High," "Proud Mary," and "What's Love Got to Do With It?" *(1939)*

Fleetwood Mac in 1972. Left to right: Mick Fleetwood, Christine McVie, **John McVie,** Stevie Nicks, Lindsey Buckingham

Tina Turner (right) in concert

Robert Goulet, singer and actor who came to fame as Sir Lancelot in the 1960 Broadway musical *Camelot,* singing "If Ever I Would Leave You." *(1933)*

Robert Goulet as Lancelot with Julie Andrews in *Camelot* (1961)

William Cowper, poet and hymnodist whose best known work, "Light Shining Out of Darkness" includes the famous phrase, "God moves in mysterious ways / His wonders to perform." *(1731)*

Performing Arts

Garcelle Beauvais, best known for roles on the TV series *The Jamie Foxx Show* and *NYPD Blue. (1966)*

Robert Adsit, actor primarily known for playing Pete, the executive producer, on the TV sitcom *30 Rock. (1965)*

Ilona Staller (Cicciolina), Italian pornographic actress elected to the Italian parliament; famously offered to have sex with Saddam Hussein in return for peace in the region. *(1951)*

Waylon Flowers, comedian and puppeteer best known for his comedy act featuring his puppet "Madame." *(1939)*

Rich Little, impressionist and voice actor nicknamed "The Man of a Thousand Voices." *(1938)*

Rich Little (right) with Ed Sullivan in a 1972 comedy skit

Ernie Coombs, starred in the long-running Canadian children's television show *Mr. Dressup. (1927)*

Religion

Saint Katharine Drexel, American heiress and philanthropist who became a nun and founded the Sisters of the Blessed Sacrament. She was canonized in 2000, the second saint born in the US and the first to have been born a US citizen. *(1858) (Photo page 18.)*

Science and Technology

Elizabeth Blackburn, shared the 2009 Nobel Prize in Physiology or Medicine as co-discoverer of telomerase. *(1948)*

Karl Ziegler, won the 1963 Nobel Prize in Chemistry for his work on polymers. *(1898)*

Norbert Wiener, MIT mathematics professor and philosopher known as the originator of the field of cybernetics. *(1894)*

Willis Carrier, American engineer who invented modern air conditioning in 1902; founded the Carrier Corporation. *(1876)*

William Derham, clergyman and natural philosopher known for creating the earliest reasonably accurate estimate of the speed of sound. *(1657)*

Social Activism

Adolfo Pérez Esquivel, Argentine artist who received the 1980 Nobel Peace Prize for his opposition to the Argentine dictatorship; he was detained, tortured, and held without trial for 14 months. *(1931)*

Bill W, co-founder of Alcoholics Anonymous, which now has over 2 million members worldwide; named one of the most important people of the 20th century by *Time* magazine. *(1895)*

Sports

Chuck Finley, 17-year baseball career as a pitcher primarily for the California Angels. His name was frequently used as an alias for the character Sam Axe on the television series *Burn Notice.* (1927)

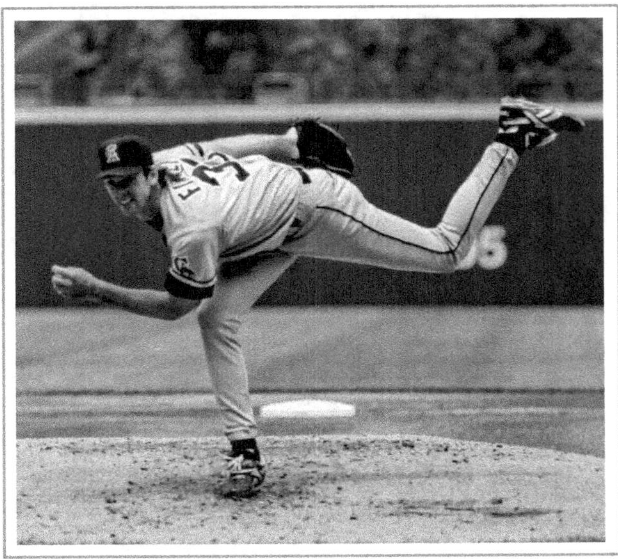

Chuck Finley (Photo: Jerry Reuss, CC BY-SA 2.0)

Dale Jarrett, NASCAR driver who won the Daytona 500 three times; member of the NASCAR Hall of Fame. *(1956)*

Harry Carson, linebacker for the New York Giants; member of the College Football Hall of Fame and the Pro Football Hall of Fame. *(1953)*

Roger Wehrli, cornerback for the St. Louis Cardinals; member of the College Football Hall of Fame and the Pro Football Hall of Fame. *(1947)*

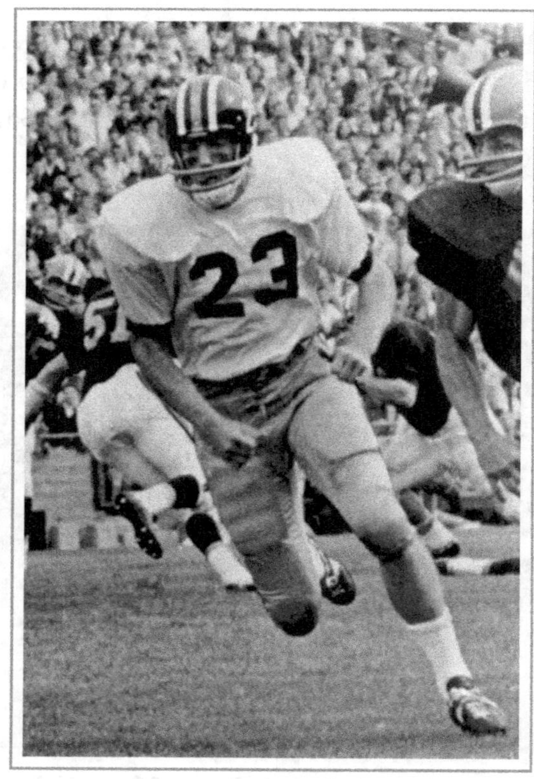

Roger Wehrli

Art Shell, NFL offensive tackle who became the first African-American head coach of the modern era; member of the College Football Hall of Fame and the Pro Football Hall of Fame. *(1946)*

Tony Verna, television sports producer credited with developing "instant replay." *(1933)*

Lefty Gomez, pitcher for the New York Yankees and the Washington Senators known for his colorful personality; member of the National Baseball Hall of Fame. *(1908)*

Lefty Gomez (1936 Goudey baseball card)

Isabella I of Castile, who financed Christopher Columbus's 1492 expedition. She died November 26, 1504

Who Died on November 26?

Activism

Sojourner Truth, African-American abolitionist and women's rights activist who escaped slavery to become a noted speaker; her most important speech was "Ain't I a Woman?" Listed in *Smithsonian* magazine as one of the 100 most significant Americans of all time. *(1883) (Photo page 16.)*

Art and Illustration

Dave Cockrum, comics artist best known as co-creator of the *X-Men* characters Nightcrawler, Storm, and Colossus. *(2006)*

Stan Berenstain, writer and illustrator best known as co-creator of the *Berenstain Bears* series of children's books. *(2005)*

Paul Rand, graphic designer known for corporate logo designs, including IBM, UPS, Westinghouse, ABC, and NeXT. *(1996)*

Engineering

John Browning, American firearms designer who created numerous classic weapons including pistols, air-cooled machine guns, and the Browning Automatic Rifle (BAR). *(1926)*

John McAdam, Scottish engineer and road-builder who developed the modern method of road construction, known as "macadamisation," which gave rise to the word "macadam." *(1836)*

Government

Isabella I of Castile, queen of Castile and wife of Ferdinand II of Aragon, whose marriage led to the political unification of Spain; best known for financing Christopher Columbus's 1492 voyage. *(1504) (Photo page 30.)*

Literature

Marguerite Henry, author of 59 books based on true stories of horses and other animals; her most famous work is the 1947 novel *Misty of Chincoteague. (1997)*

Adam Mickiewicz, widely regarded as Poland's greatest poet. Works include the poetic drama *Dziady* and the national epic poem *Pan Tadeusz. (1855)*

Military

Silvestre S. Herrera, received the Medal of Honor as a US Army private during World War II for a one-man charge against an enemy stronghold that captured eight soldiers, immediately followed by a single-handed attack across a minefield in which he lost both his legs while continuing to provide covering machine gun fire. *(2007)*

Thomas Lanphier Jr., US Army Air Force fighter pilot who shared credit with Rex Barber for shooting down the Japanese bomber carrying Admiral Isoroku Yamamoto. *(1987)*

Edward "Butch" O'Hare, first Navy fighter ace of World War II and first World War II Navy recipient of the Medal of Honor; namesake of Chicago's O'Hare Airport. *(1943)*

Lieutenant Edward "Butch" O'Hare in his Grumman F4F Wildcat

Music

Tommy Dorsey, jazz trombonist and bandleader in the Big Band era; biggest hits include "I'll Never Smile Again" and "I'm Getting Sentimental Over You." *(1956) (Photo page 34.)*

Bandleader brothers **Tommy Dorsey** (left) and Jimmy Dorsey"

Performing Arts

Fritz Weaver, actor who appeared in such films as *Fail Safe, Marathon Man, Creepshow,* and *The Thomas Crown Affair. (2016)*

Tony Musante, actor best known as the lead in the 1970s series *Toma. (2013)*

Jane Kean, actress and singer best known for playing Trixie Norton in the 1960s version of *The Honeymooners* and as the voice of Belle in the perennial Christmas television special *Mister Magoo's Christmas Carol. (2013)*

Mel Tolkin, television comedy head writer for the 1950s sketch comedy series *Your Show of Shows. (2007)*

Philippe de Broca, French director of such films as *That Man from Rio* and *King of Hearts. (2004)*

Science

Joseph Murray, surgeon who performed the first successful human kidney transplant; shared the 1990 Nobel Prize in Physiology or Medicine for his work in transplantation. *(2012)*

Sports

Guy Lewis, basketball player and coach named to the National Collegiate Basketball Hall of Fame and the Naismith Memorial Basketball Hall of Fame. *(2007)*

Bob Johnson, ice hockey coach at collegiate and professional levels; member of the Hockey Hall of Fame. *(1991)*

Quote of the Day

"Sometimes I lie awake at night and I ask, 'Why me?' And the voice says, 'Nothing personal; your name just happened to come up."

Charles M. Schulz, creator of *Peanuts*
born November 26, 1922

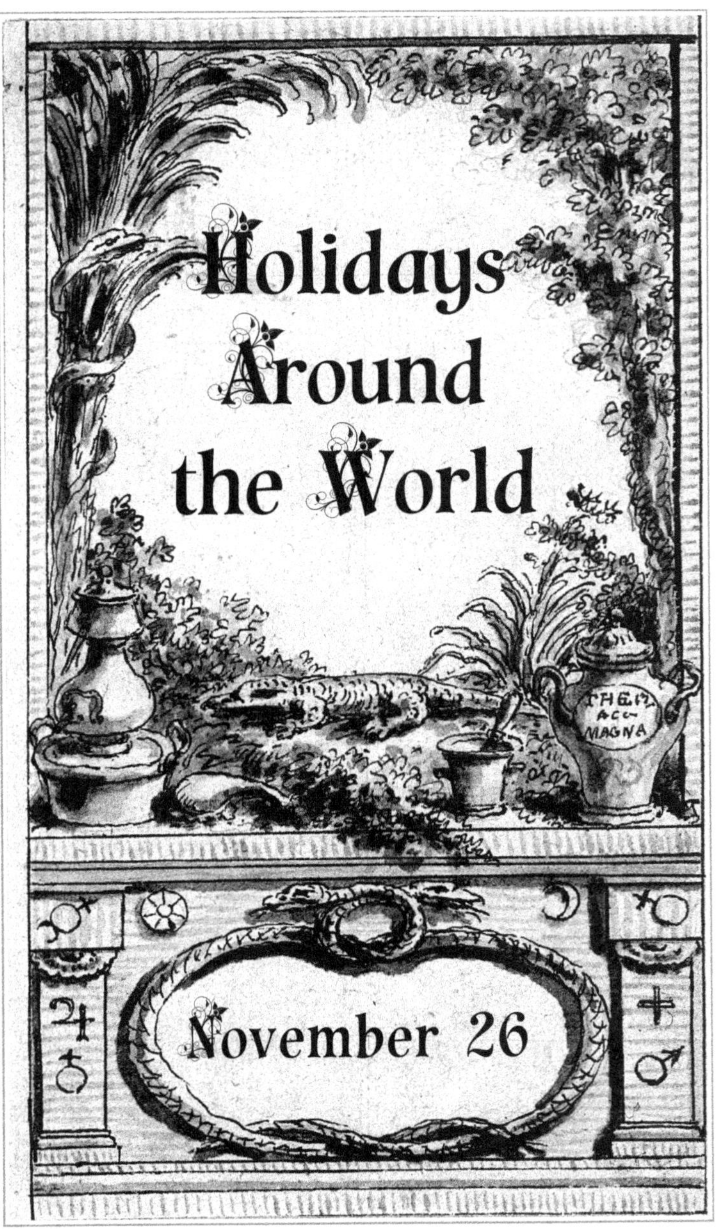
Holidays
Around
the World

THER
AC
MAGNA

November 26

Detail from "The First Thanksgiving," by Jean Leon Gerome Ferris

Thanksgiving

Ceremonies of giving thanks are part of many religions and many cultures. In some countries, the United States and Canada among them, a formal Thanksgiving Day for the nation has become a major annual holiday.

A Brief History of Thanksgiving

The origins of Thanksgiving Day in the United States and Canada trace back to the English Reformation, which instituted special Days of Thanksgiving to celebrate such events as the British victory against the Spanish Armada. One such Thanksgiving, begun in 1606, turned into the British Guy Fawkes Day.

It's unclear which Thanksgiving Day came first. Some trace the first Canadian Thanksgiving to 1578 and the explorer Martin Frobisher. In the United States, the origin of Thanksgiving is generally traced to a Pilgrim feast in 1621. As in England, Thanksgiving wasn't an automatic annual event, but happened only when declared by royal governors and later by the Continental Congress. Some Thanksgiving Days were celebrated only in a single state; others nationwide.

In both countries, Thanksgiving slowly became a standard public holiday. Canada's official Thanksgiving Day *(Jour de l'action de grâce)* began in 1872, though it wasn't until 1957 that it settled on its current date of the second Monday of October.

(October 8 through October 14, same day as Columbus Day in the US.)

In the United States, each state set its own Thanksgiving Day, but by the beginning of the 19th century, it was mostly on the final Thursday of November. Abraham Lincoln made it official in 1863. In 1941, however, Congress changed the date to make Thanksgiving the *fourth* Thursday of November rather than the *final* one, because some years that would leave too few days for Christmas shopping. That's why in the United States Thanksgiving Day can fall on any day from *November 22 to November 28.*

Thanksgiving in North America

Although Thanksgiving is often celebrated with prayers and proclamations, it isn't a formal religious holiday and so most rituals are secular in nature. North American celebrations normally include a large family dinner, with turkey as the traditional featured dish.

Thanksgiving dinner extends to charity as well, with many volunteering to make and serve dinner to those in need. There are several major parades, with the Macy's Thanksgiving Day Parade the best known in the US, and the Kitchener-Waterloo Oktoberfest parade in Canada. And, of course, there's football.

Families often get together, making the Thanksgiving holidays one of the busiest travel periods of the year, especially in the US.

A Thanksgiving dream from *Little Nemo in Slumberland*, by Winsor McCay (1905)

Thanksgiving in Other Countries

Different versions of Thanksgiving Day can be found around the world.

Some places have a Thanksgiving Day connected to the North American traditions. The Pieterskirk (St. Peter's Church) in the Dutch city of Leiden has a nondenominational religious service on *the morning of the American Thanksgiving* because many of the Pilgrims had lived in Leiden, and had recorded marriages, births, and deaths in the Pieterskerk (St. Peter's Church).

While Australia as a whole doesn't celebrate Thanksgiving, the external Australian territory Norfolk Island does. American whaling ships brought the celebration to that island, though they celebrate it on the last Wednesday of November. (*November 24 to November 30*).

The Philippines adopted Thanksgiving when it was an American colony, but the tradition eventually faded out.

Liberia, colonized by freed black slaves from the United States, celebrates its Thanksgiving on the first Thursday of November (*November 1-7*).

In the Caribbean, Grenada celebrates Thanksgiving Day on *October 25*, the anniversary of the US-led invasion of the island in 1983 that deposed the then-current government. Saint Lucia celebratess the *first Monday in October (October 1-7).*

In the United Kingdom, there is a Harvest Festival of Thanksgiving, but that does not have a fixed date. It's traditionally held on or near the Sunday of the harvest moon that occurs closest to the autumnal equinox, which essentially means *sometime in late September or early October*, usually close to Canadian Thanksgiving. Harvest festivals are celebrated in many countries; a complete list can be found on Wikipedia.

Germany holds religious ceremonies associated with *Erntedankfest*, in early October. Japan has a Labor Thanksgiving Day (勤労感謝の日, or *Kinrō Kansha no Hi*), established during the American post-World War II occupation, which commemorates labor and production and giving one another thanks. It comes from an early celebration that honored hard work.

Whatever and however you give thanks, a very happy Thanksgiving to one and all!

Marie Antoinette by Marie Louise Élisabeth Vigée LeBrun (1783) —
for **NATIONAL CAKE DAY**

More Holidays and Celebrations

If you're looking for a reason to take your special day off, you should know that every single day is a holiday somewhere in the world! Here's some of what you can celebrate on November 26!

November 26 General Events

Anti-Obesity Day (India and some Gulf states)

Various health care organizations mark November 26 as Anti-Obesity Day, highlighting obesity as a public health hazard.

День Конституции Республики Абхазии (Abkhazia)

Abkhazia, a partially recognized state that broke away from Georgia, celebrates Constitution Day to commemorate the adoption of their constitution on November 26, 1994.

Samvidhan Divas (India)

Constitution Day in India commemorates the November 26, 1949, adoption of the Constitution of India.

Uls Tunhaglasnii Üdür (Mongolia)

Mongolia celebrates Republic Day (Улс тунхагласны өдөр) on November 26.

November 26 Food Holidays

National Cake Day (US)

In the United States, almost every day of the year is dedicated to a particular food. (Some other countries do this also, but not every day.) Sponsored by manufacturers, retailers, farmers, or simply fans, these days are often proclaimed by the President, Congress, state governors, or mayors. Given that there are more different foods than days of the year, some days honor more than one kind of food!

November 26 is **National Cake Day**. The origin of cakes dates back to ancient Rome, when eggs, butter, and sometimes honey were added to bread. In parts of Britain, "cake" means a biscuit made of oatmeal.

Although the saying "Let them eat cake" (*Qu'ils mangent de la brioche*) is attributed to Marie Antoinette *(previous page)*, there's actually no record of her ever having said it. The phrase appeared in the autobiography of Jean-Jacques Rousseau, which was published when Marie Antoinette was only nine years old. The wife of Louis XVI, Maria Theresa, was also cited as having used the phrase nearly 100 years before Marie Antoinette was born. In fact, Marie Antoinette was known as a patron of charity and support for the poor, so it's particularly unlikely she would have ever used the phrase.

A Cake (Photo: Alfred Cheney Johnston)

Honorary Food Months

In addition, the entire month of November is used to celebrate numerous foods. Here's a list of what to eat in the month of November!

- National Georgia Pecan Month
- National Peanut Butter Lover's Month
- National Pepper Month
- National Pomegranate Month
- National Raisin Bread Month
- Sweet Potato Awareness Month
- Vegan Month
- National Fun With Fondue Month

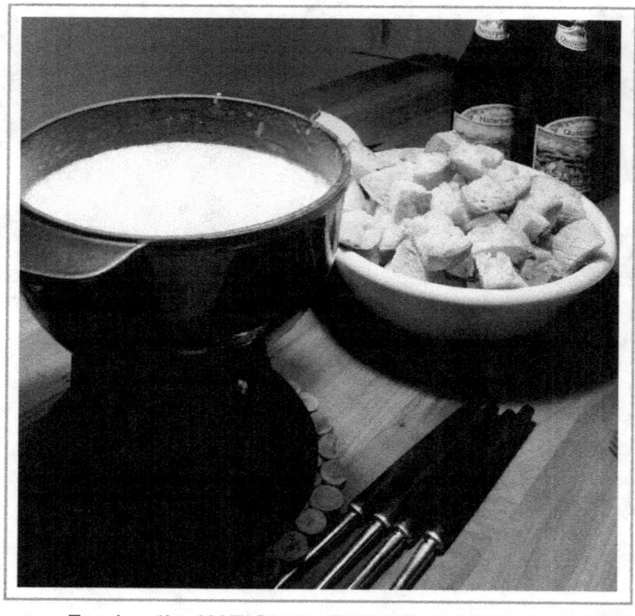

Cheese Fondue (for **NATIONAL FUN WITH FONDUE MONTH**).
(The Junes/Zitroenesspresse, CC BY-SA 2.0)

Religious Feast Days and Holidays

Saint Days

Each day in the year is considered a feast day for one or more saints. In Western Christianity, November 26 is the feast day of Saints John Berchmans, Pope Siricius, Sylvester Gozzolini, and Isaac Watts (Episcopal Church USA).

In Eastern (Orthodox) Christianity, it is also the feast of Saints Peter of Jerusalem, Procopius of Persia, Amator, Basolus, Martin of Arades, Conrad of Constance, Vacz, Innocent of Irkutsk, and Stylianos of Paphlagonia. (These saints are commemorated on November 13 by "Old Calendrists.*)

Saint Stylianos of Paphlagonia (Photo: Wolfymoza, CC BY-SA 4.0)

---

* Old Calendrists use the Julian calendar, rather than the more modern Gregorian calendar, for liturgical purposes. "New Style" November 26 is the Gregorian equivalent of "Old Style" November 1. For more on different calendar types, see "What Day of the Week is November 26?"

Moveable and Multi-Day Events

Some events take place over a specific week or time period. Start and finish dates may vary from year to year. Some events occur on different days each year (such as "fourth Saturday of a month"). These events sometimes include or take place on November 26.

Week-Long Celebrations

- Anti-Bullying Week *(UK, 3rd week in November)*
- Geography Awareness Week *(3rd week in November)*
- International Bible Week *(week beginning the Sunday before Thanksgiving)*
- National Farm-City Week *(week that ends on Thanksgiving Day)*
- National Family Week *(week including Thanksgiving Day)*
- National Games Week *(week including Thanksgiving Day)*
- Sixteen Days of Activism Against Gender-Based Violence *(November 25 to December 10)*

Moveable events that sometimes fall on November 26 include (US unless otherwise specified):

- Black Friday *(beginning of the Christmas shopping season, day after Thanksgiving)*
- Cyber Monday *(Monday after Thanksgiving, created to persuade people to shop online)*
- Flossing Day *(day after Thanksgiving)*

- Harvest Festival *(Turkmenistan, last Sunday in November)*
- National Adoption Day *(Saturday before the 4th Thursday)*
- National Day of Listening *(day after Thanksgiving)*
- Native American Heritage Day *(day after Thanksgiving)*
- You're Welcomegiving Day *(day after Thanksgiving)*
- Small Business Saturday *(Saturday after Thanksgiving)*

Eager **BLACK FRIDAY** shoppers (Photo: Powhusku, CC BY-SA 2.0)

November Honorary Months

Presidents, Congresses, and nations around the world issue proclamations recognizing particular months to honor certain causes. These events generally fall in October, though honorary months do come and go. Holidays established by states and nonprofit organizations are listed if verified.

If not otherwise specified, all months are US. There is some variation from year to year; some celebratory months get added and others get dropped. Two places to get up to date information are the current edition of *Chase's Calendar of Events* or the website Brownielocks. Here are some honorary designations for November.

- Adopt a Turkey Month *(photo next page)*
- Aviation History Month
- Epilepsy Awareness Month
- Historic Bridge Awareness Month
- Military Family Appreciation Month
- National Adoption Month
- National Diabetes Month
- National Family Literacy Month
- National Hospice Month
- National Memoir Writing Month
- National Novel Writing Month (NaNoWriMo)
- World Sponge Month

Deček's Puranom, by Almanach (National Gallery of Slovenia — for
ADOPT A TURKEY MONTH

Quote of the Day

"November's night is dark and drear,
The dullest month of all the year."

Letitia Elizabeth Landon,
in *Traits and Trials of Early Life* (1836)

# About the Month of November

November, by Joachim von Sandrart

November: The Eleventh Month

When shrieked
The bleak November winds, and smote the woods,
And the brown fields were herbless, and the shades
That met above the merry rivulet
Were spoiled, I sought, I loved them still; they seemed
Like old companions in adversity.

William Cullen Bryant, A Winter Piece

In Latin, *novem* means "nine," so it may seem strange that November is the eleventh month of the year. The original Roman calendar started in March, making November indeed the ninth month. No one is completely sure when the start of the year was moved to January, but the traditional name of November stuck.

In the northern hemisphere, November is a month in late autumn. In the southern hemisphere, November is in the springtime. May is its opposite month; spring in the north and fall in the south.

If it's not a Leap Year, November always starts on the same day of the week as February. If it is a leap year, November starts on the same day of the week as March.

November in Other Cultures

The month of November has different names in different languages. Some nations use calendars other than the Gregorian, and their months may overlap with November. In lunar-based calendars, such as the Islamic calendar, months move through the seasons. Still, many languages often have a word for November itself.

Arabic: نوفمبر (Nūfambar)

Chinese and Japanese: 十一月

Croatian: Studeni

Czech and Polish: Listopad

Finnish: Marraskuu

Greek: Νοέμβριος

Hebrew: נובמבר

Hindi: नवंबर

Old English: Blōtmōnaþ

Russian: ноябрь

November Sayings and Superstitions

Here are some sayings and superstitions associated with the month of November

- "A November bride will be liberal and kind, but sometimes cold."
- "Married in veils of November mist/Fortune your wedding ring has kissed."
- "If you wed in bleak November, only joys will come, remember."

November, by Eugène Grasset

November Symbols

Birthstone: Topaz (primarily yellow), and citrine. Topaz is associated with strength, tenacity, dedication and resilience. Citrine is supposed to encourage vitality and promote good health.

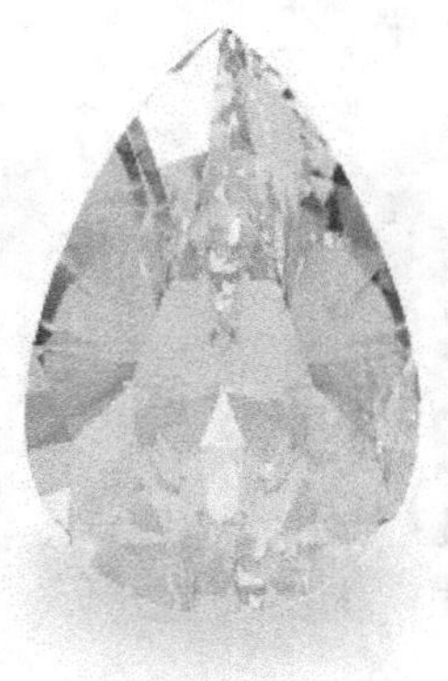

Citrine

Birth Flower: Chrysanthemum. The Chrysanthemum is associated with compassion, friendship,and joy. Red is for love, white for innocence, and yellow for unrequited love.

Chrysanthemums, by Claude Monet

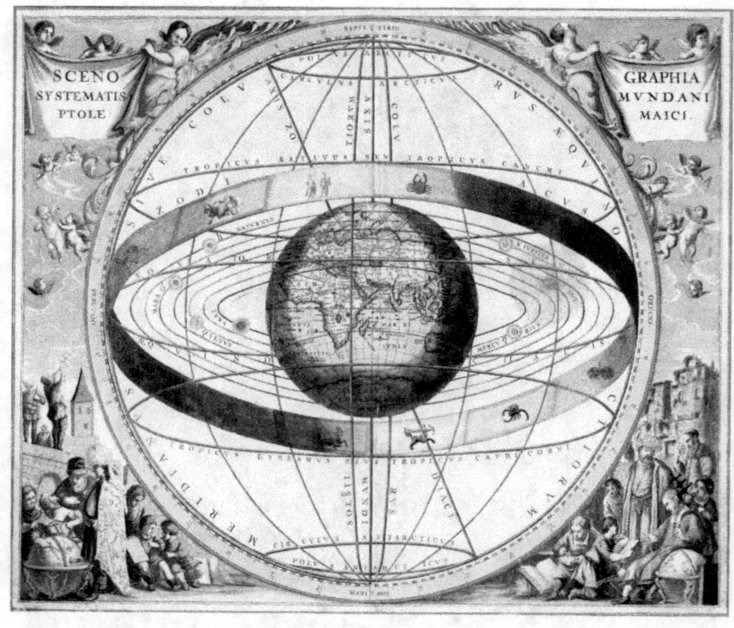

Scenography of the Ptolemaic Cosmography, by Johannes van Loon, based on Andreas Cellarius's *Harmonia Macrocosmica,* 1660

November 26 Zodiac Signs

From the perspective of someone on Earth, the Sun appears to move through the sky throughout the year, along a path astronomers call the *ecliptic plane*. The ecliptic plane is divided into twelve constellations, known as the zodiac, based on traditionally observed patterns of stars. On your birthday, you can't see your constellation, because it's in the daytime sky.

The zodiac was first developed by Babylonian astronomers about 2,500 years ago. Because they were unaware that the Earth wobbles like a spinning top (known as *precession*), they didn't make allowance for the fact that the Sun's path through the zodiac changes over time.

That means there are now two sets of dates for your birth sign. The *tropical dates* are the original Babylonian dates; the *sidereal dates* tell you where the Sun actually appears as it moves along its annual path.

For November 26, the tropical sign is **Sagittarius** and the sidereal sign is **Scorpio**.

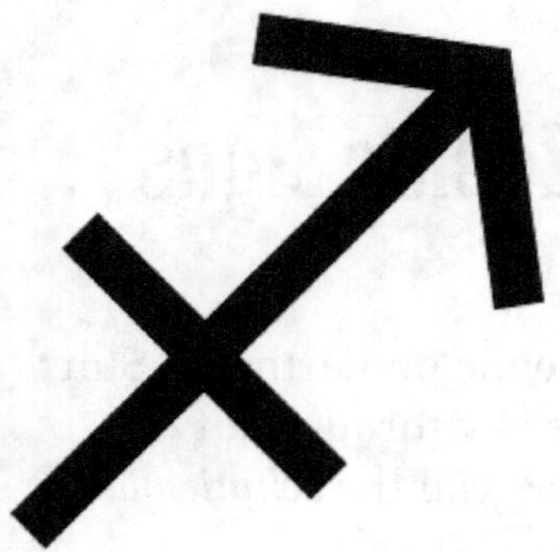

Sagittarius

Tropical November 23 to December 21
Sidereal December 16 to January 14

The centaur (half-man, half-horse) Chiron was famous as a healer and as an archer. He tutored Achilles, Jason (of Argonaut fame), and Hercules. Unfortunately for Chiron, Hercules accidentally shot him with an arrow that had been dipped in hydra poison. He was unable to find a cure, so gave up his immortality to free Prometheus, and died. In recognition of his sacrifice, Zeus placed him among the stars.

In astrology, Sagittarians are known for their independence and craving for adventure and excitement. They are encouraging and kind, but sometimes lack commitment. They are supposed to be compatible with Aries, Leo, and Libra, but not with Taurus, Scorpio, or Capricorn.

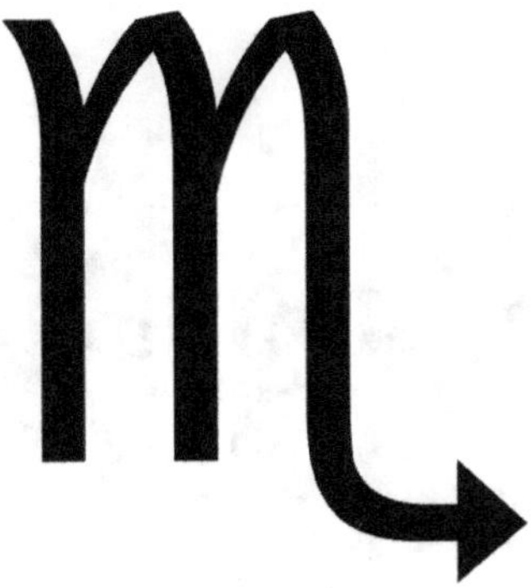

Scorpio

Tropical October 23 to November 21
Sidereal November 16 to December 15

Scorpio, the Scorpion, appears in the Greek myth of the hunter Orion. Because Orion had touched the robes of the goddess Artemis, in revenge, the goddess had the scorpion kill Orion. As a reward, she placed the scorpion in the sky, where it chases Orion through the eternal night.

Scorpio is a fire sign, and people born under this sign are supposed to be determined, reserved, loyal, and secretive. Scorpios are supposed to be compatible with the water signs of Pisces and Capricorn.

Illustration by Edward Penfield

What Day of the Week is November 26?

On what day of the week does November 26 fall?

Surprisingly, this isn't an easy question. Because the calendar year is 365 days long (366 in leap years), it doesn't divide evenly by the seven days of the week.

Also, the Earth goes around the Sun in about 365-1/4 days, so a calendar tends to drift over time. That's why the same date falls on different weekdays in different years.

This is made even more complicated by a change in calendars that took place in 1582. Our modern calendar has its roots in ancient Rome, in a calendar reform conducted by Julius Caesar. Caesar commissioned mathematicians to attack the problem, and they came up with the idea of leap years, and thus standardized the calendar for centuries to come. This was called the Julian calendar.

Over time, however, the small errors in Caesar's calculation compounded. That's why Pope Gregory XIII commissioned the Gregorian calendar, used in most of the world today. Some countries converted in 1582, when the calendar was first developed; some converted later; other still haven't changed.

Gregorian and Julian aren't the only types of calendars. The Hebrew year, the Islamic year, and many other calendars are used in different parts of the world and among different people.

You can convert Gregorian dates to other calendars, including the Hebrew calendar, the Islamic calendar, and even the Mayan calendar by visiting the Fourmilab Calendar Converter at http://www.fourmilab.ch/documents/calendar/.

Chinese calendar systems are quite complex and have changed several times; a full discussion is far beyond the scope of this book. If you're interested, you can find information here: http://www.hermetic.ch/cal_stud/chinese_cal.htm.

On Names and Dates

Historians use "CE" (Common Era) and "BCE" (Before the Common Era) instead of the more common "AD" (Anno Domini, or Year of Our Lord) and "BC" (Before Christ), reflecting the fact that the year-numbering system established by the Gregorian calendar is used throughout the world in many countries not culturally Christian.

The CE/BCE designation dates back to at least 1708, and has been adopted as a standard by the United Nations and the Universal Postal Union. Because this series of books covers events and people of all nations and cultures, we use the CE/BCE terms.

The abbreviation "O.S." ("Old Style") on some dates refers to the fact that the Russian Empire did not switch from the Julian to the Gregorian calendar at the same time as the rest of Europe, and therefore some figures and events have two dates.

Also, in the Julian calendar in England in the 16th century, the year began on March 25 rather than January 1. To avoid confusion with Gregorian dates, dates between January and March were often written using both years.

People and events whose original names are not in the Western alphabet have their native names (where possible) in the appropriate script shown in parenthesis. If you are using an e-reader to access an electronic version of this book, all characters don't always display on all devices.

A 50-year brass perpetual calendar.

Quote of the Day

"Time is an illusion, lunchtime doubly so."

Douglas Adams,
from *The Hitchhiker's Guide to the Galaxy*

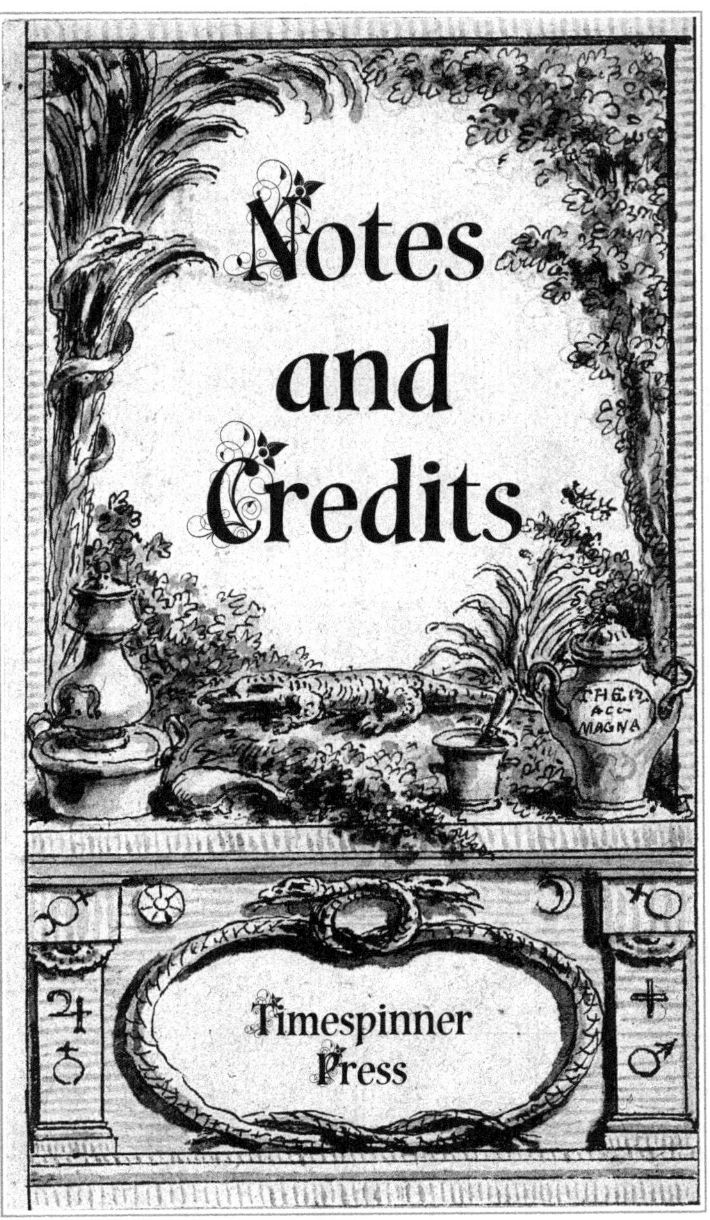
Notes
and
Credits
Timespinner
Press

Cartoon by John T. McCutcheon

Copyright, Credit, and Contact

Follow Us

Our blog "This Day in History" (http://
timespinnerpress.com/this-day-in-history/) features short
articles on events and people associated with each day, and
updates several times each week. Also subscribe to the
"Quote of the Day" at http://timespinnerpress.com/quote-
of-the-day/. You can get daily links by following us on
Facebook at TimespinnerPress, or on Twitter as
@sidewisethinker.

Contact Us

Find an error or a format problem? Want information about
the series, about us, or about when the volume for your
special day might be available? Please email us at
editor@timespinnerpress.com. (We also take requests if your
special day isn't yet complete. Please give us at least six
weeks' notice if possible.)

Sources

We owe a great debt to Wikipedia, which is our first stop for
research. We attempt to make independent confirmation of
all important dates and facts through a variety of other
sources.

Other sources we frequently use include the Library of
Congress; "on this day" listings from *Encyclopedia Britannica*,
the *New York Times*, and the BBC; Omniglot for the names of
months in other languages; *Chase's Calendar of Events*; and, of
course, the always essential Google.

All art and photographs are either in the public domain, used under a Creative Commons license, or with a "fair use" justification, and most frequently come from Wikimedia Commons and the Library of Congress Prints and Photographs Division.

Attribution is provided where possible, or as requested by the copyright owner, or when there is particular historical significance, listed below. For information about any particular illustration or photograph, please contact us.

Credits

1. The 2012 photograph of the golden mask of Tutankhamun in the Egyptian Museum was taken by Carsten Frenzl, and is used here under CC BY-SA 2.0.

2. The illustration of the month of November used on the back cover is from the French Gothic illuminated manuscript *Les Très Riches Heures du duc de Berry* by the Limbourg Brothers, Jean Colombe, and an intermediate painter whose name is lost to history. It is in the public domain because its copyright has expired.

3. The box graphic used on the first page is from a 1916 pamphlet entitled "Divorce versus Democracy" authored by G. K. Chesterton, originally published in London by the Society of St. Peter and St. Paul. It is in the public domain in the US because it was published prior to 1923, and is in the public domain in all countries (including the country of origin) in which the copyright time is the author's life plus 70 years or less.

4. The graphic design for the section pages in this book is from a design originally created for a pharmacy label. It is courtesy of Wellcome Images (ICV No 11073, photo V0010813), and is used here under CC BY-SA 4.0.

5. The painting "November" from *Labors of the Month* by Simon Bening, was originally published in the first half of the 16th century, and is in the public domain because its copyright has expired.

6. The 1922 photograph of the opening of the tomb of Pharaoh Tutankhamun was taken by Harry Burton. It is in the public domain because it was first published in the US prior to January 1, 1923.

7. The 1922 photograph of the entrance to Pharaoh Tutankhamun's tomb was taken by Harry Burton. It is in the public domain because it was first published in the US prior to January 1, 1923.

8. The 1922 photograph of Howard Carter in Pharaoh Tutankhamun's burial chamber was taken by Harry Burton. It is in the public domain because it was first published in the US prior to January 1, 1923.

9. The 16th century portrait of Vlad the Impaler is by an unknown artist. It is in the public domain because its copyright has expired.

10. The 1942 trailer screenshot from *Casablanca* is in the public domain because it was first published in the US between 1923 and 1977 without a copyright notice. Traditionally, film trailers are not copyrighted because of the way they are intended to be used.

11. The 2003 photograph of the final Concorde flight was taken by Adrian Pingstone, who released the work into the public domain.

12. The 1864 photograph of Sojourner Truth is in the public domain because its copyright has expired. The image is courtesy Google Art Project.

13. The first *Peanuts* comic strip is copyright © 2005 by United Features Syndicate, and is used here under "fair use" provisions of US copyright law. No free alternative can exist because the characters are copyrighted and trademarked. It is a low-resolution image not suitable for the creation of counterfeit merchandise or the creation of illegal copies, it does not limit the copyright owner's rights to sell the comic strip in any way, and it is a significant image of a world-famous cartoonist used for the purpose of identification.

14. The 1883 photograph of the Dodge City Peace Commission is in the public domain because its copyright has expired.

15. The 1911 photograph of Mary Edwards Walker by George Grantham Bain is in the public domain according the the

Library of Congress. It is from the George Grantham Bain collection at the Library, with digital ID ggbain.25626.

16. The 1977 trade ad for the Fleetwood Mac album *Rumours* first appeared in *Billboard*, June 25, 1977 issue, page 86. It is in the public domain because it was first published in the US between 1923 and 1977 without a copyright notice.

17. The 1972 photograph of Tina Turner in concert was taken by Heinrich Klaffs, and is used here under CC BY-SA 2.0.

18. The 1961 publicity photo from *Camelot* is in the public domain because it was first published in the US between 1923 and 1977 without a copyright notice.

19. The 1972 publicity photograph from the *ABC Comedy Hour* is in the public domain because it was first published in the US between 1923 and 1977 without a copyright notice. Traditionally, publicity photographs are not copyrighted because of the way they are intended to be used.

20. The 1996 photograph of Chuck Finley was taken by Jerry Reuss, and is used here under CC BY-SA 2.0.

21. The 1967 photograph of Roger Wehrli is in the public domain because it was first published in the US between 1923 and 1977 without a copyright notice.

22. The 1936 Goudey baseball card of Lefty Gomez is in the public domain because it was published in the US between 1923 and 1953, and although there may or may not have been a copyright notice, the copyright was not renewed.

23. The painting of Isabella I of Castile attributed to Gerard David was created circa 1520 and is in the public domain because its copyright has expired.

24. The 1942 photograph of Lt. Butch O'Hare is in the public domain because it was taken by an employee of the US government as part of that person's official duties.

25. The 1955 publicity photograph of Tommy and Jimmy Dorsey is in the public domain because it was first published in the US between 1923 and 1977 without a copyright notice.

26. The painting "The First Thanksgiving" by Jean Leon Gerome Farris was created between 1912 and 1915 as part of the series *The Pageant of a Nation*, and is available from the Library of Congress Prints and Photographs Division under

digital ID cph.3g04961 It is in the public domain because its copyright has expired. The image has been cropped

27. The 1905 Thanksgiving comic strip from *Little Nemo in Slumberland* by Winsor McCay is in the public domain in the United States because it was published or registered with the US Copyright Office before January 1, 1923.

28. The 1910 Thanksgiving postcard was published by Wolf & Co., New York. It is in the public domain because its copyright has expired.

29. The 1783 portrait of Marie Antoinette by Marie Louise Élisabeth Vigée LeBrun is in the public domain because its copyright has expired. It can be found in the collection of Prince Ludwig von Hessen und bei Rhein in Wolfsgarten Castle, Germany.

30. The pre-1920 photograph of a cake by Alfred Cheney Johnston is in the public domain because its copyright has expired.

31. The 2009 photograph of cheese fondue is by "The Junes" and modified by "Zitronenpresse."It is used here under CC BY-SA 2.0.

32. The 2016 photograph of a painting of Saint Stylianos is by "Wolfymoza," and is used here under CC BY-SA 4.0.)

33. The 2013 photograph of Black Friday shoppers is by "Powhusku," and is used here under CC BY-SA 2.0. It has been cropped.

34. The 17th century painting *Deček's Puranom* by Almanach is from the collection of the National Gallery of Slovenia (NGS3100). It is in the public domain because its copyright has expired.

35. The painting "November" by Joachim von Sandrart was created in 1643, and is in the public domain because its copyright has expired. The original can be seen in the Staatsgalerie im Neuen Schloss, Schleißheim, Austria

36. The 1896 postcard "November" by Eugène Grasset is in the public domain because its copyright has expired.

37. The photograph of a citrine is by Les Facettes and is used here under CC BY-SA 3.0.

38. The 1882 painting of chrysanthemums by Claude Monet is in the public domain because its copyright has expired. The

painting is in the collection of the Metropolitan Museum of Art, New York.

39. The celestial sphere is from *Scenography of the Ptolemaic Cosmography,* by Johannes van Loon, based on Andreas Cellarius's *Harmonia Macrocosmica,* 1660. It is in the public domain because its copyright has expired.

40. The 1906 automobile calendar is by Edward Penfield, and is in the collection of the Library of Congress Prints and Photographs Division. It is in the public domain because its copyright has expired.

41. The 50-year perpetual calendar photograph is in the public domain.

42. The cartoon by John T. McCutcheon is from his 1905 collection *The Mysterious Stranger and Other Cartoons by John T. McCutcheon.* It is in the public domain because its copyright has expired.

43. The 1879 painting "November" by John Grimshaw is in the public domain because its copyright has expired.

44. The painting "November" is from the *Brevarium Grimani,* circa 1510, and is in the public domain because its copyright has expired.

License Description and Terms

Aside from material purely in the public domain, photographs and other material in this book are used under specific licenses permitting free use, usually with an attribution requirement. For full text and terms of these licenses, click or enter the appropriate links below. If you believe there is an error in the copyright status or attribution of any of these images, please email us.

- Creative Commons Attribution 2.0 Generic (CC-BY 2.0): http://creativecommons.org/licenses/by/2.0/deed.en
- Creative Commons Attribution-Share Alike 3.0 Generic (CC-BY-SA 3.0): http://creativecommons.org/licenses/by-sa/3.0/
- Creative Commons Attribution-Share Alike 2.5 Generic (CC-BY-SA 2.5): http://creativecommons.org/licenses/by-sa/2.5/deed.en
- Creative Commons Attribution-Share Alike 2.0 Generic (CC-BY-SA 2.0): http://creativecommons.org/licenses/by/2.0/deed.en
- Creative Commons Attribution-Share Alike 1.0 Generic (CC-BY-SA 1.0): http://creativecommons.org/licenses/by-sa/1.0/deed.en
- CC0 1.0 Universal (CC0 1.0) Public Domain Dedication (CC0 1.0) http://creativecommons.org/publicdomain/zero/1.0/deed.en
- GNU Free Documentation License (GFDL): http://en.wikipedia.org/wiki/Wikipedia:Text_of_the_GNU_Free_Documentation_License
- License Art Libre (Free Art License): http://artlibre.org

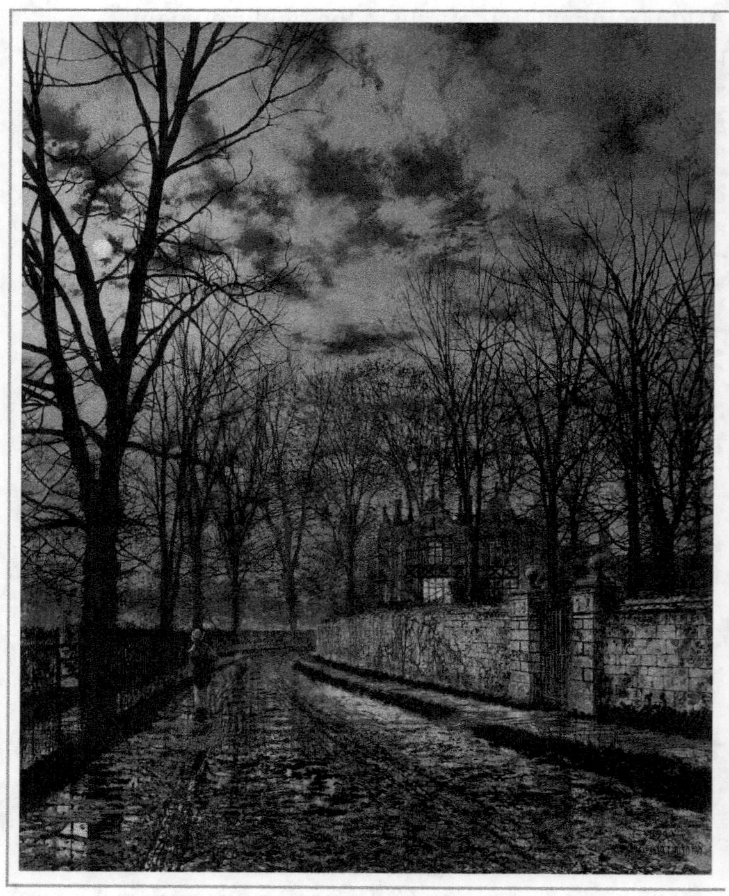

November, by John Atkinson Grimshaw

Other Books from Timespinner Press

The Story of a Special Day

Michael Dobson

A series of (eventually) 366 volumes covering everything that happened on your special day! Events, births, deaths, quotes, holidays, and much more. It's like a birthday card they'll never throw away!

US$7.95 print/US$2.99 ebook.

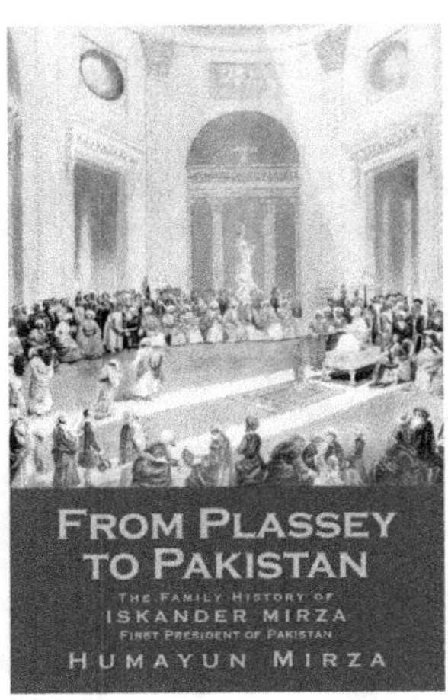

From Plassey to Pakistan

Humayun Mirza

The history of British Colonial India and the formation of Pakistan from the unique perspective of the son of Pakistan's first president and last of the royal line of Bengal, Bihar, and Orissa! This unique historical document tells the inside story of this distinguished family, including the detailed story of the coup that toppled his father from power!

US$27.95 print

A Whole New Navy: America's War in the Pacific

Miles Durr

The most comprehensive and detailed description of America's naval war in the Pacific ever—every battle, every ship, every task force and every task group from Pearl Harbor through the Japanese surrender! A must-have for the collection of every World War II buff!

US$29.95 print

Improbable History: The Weird, the Obscure, and the Strangely Important

edited by Michael Dobson

From the birth of Western civilization to the rescue of Apollo 13, from the Leaning Tower of Pisa to Florence's Duomo, history has often turned on small, improbable details. Whatever happened to the ancient Samaritan people? Why did a fortuitous rainstorm allow the British to conquer India? How did an air raid in Italy lead to the development of chemotherapy? What happened when Albert Einstein met Adolf Hitler on the streets of Berlin? How did the Japanese manage to attack the US mainland using balloons? A cast of award-winning writers tackle some of the strangest tales in history!

US$19.95 print

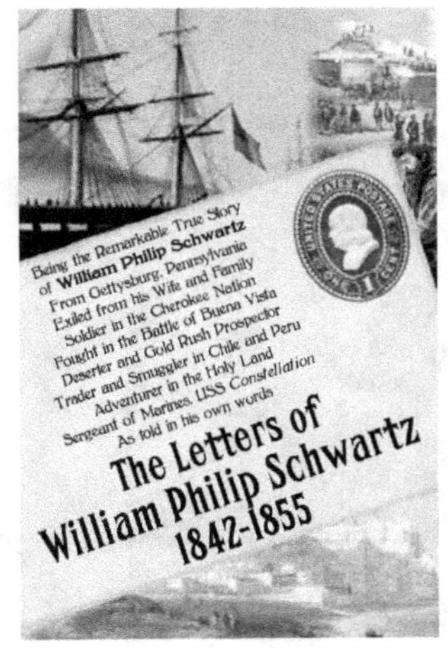

The Letters of William Philip Schwartz 1842-1855

edited by John F. Schwartz

The 19th century soldier and adventurer William Philip Schwartz wrote a series of vivid and detailed letters chronicling his adventures in the Indian Wars, the Mexican-American War, the Gold Rush, and his term as Marine sergeant aboard the USS Constellation. A pioneer in photography, he took *the first known war photographs*. An unforgettable first-hand look into life in the 19th century!

US$17.95 print

Timespinner
Press

www.timespinnerpress.com

November, from the *Brevarium Grimani* (c.1510)